JB   HOLMES, PARKER.
TEB   TIM TEBOW.

WITHDRAWN

Eas
,
East

FOOTBALL'S RISING STARS
TIM TEBOW

Parker Holmes

PowerKiDS press

New York

Published in 2013 by The Rosen Publishing Group, Inc.
29 East 21st Street, New York, NY 10010

First Edition

Editor: Matt Monteverde
Book Design: Matt Monteverde

Photo Credits: Garrett Ellwood/Getty Images, p. 5 Orlando Sentinel/MCT via Getty Images p. 7, Doug Benc/Getty Images, p. 9 Kelly Kline/Getty Images, p. 11 Kevin C. Cox/Getty Images, p. 13 Justin Edmonds/Getty Images, p. 15 Garrett Ellwood/Getty Images, p. 17 Jeff Gross/Getty Images, p. 19 Ezra Shaw/Getty Images, p. 21 Al Messerschmidt/Getty Images, p. 22-23, Streeter Lecka/Getty Images, p. 24, Sam Greenwood/Getty Images, and Doug Pensinger/Getty Images, Front Cover Patrick Smith/Getty Images, Doug Pensinger/Getty Images, and Al Messerschmidt/Getty Images, Back Cover

Library of Congress Cataloging-in-Publication Data

Holmes, Parker.
 Tim Tebow / by Parker Holmes. – 1st ed.
    p. cm. – (Football's rising stars)
 Includes index.
 ISBN 978-1-4488-9191-7 (library binding) – ISBN 978-1-4488-9206-8 (pbk.) – ISBN 978-1-4488-9207-5 (6-pack)
 1. Tebow, Tim, 1987- 2. Football players–United States–Biography. 3. Quarterbacks (Football)–United States–Biography. I. Title.
 GV939.T423H65 2013
 796.332092–dc23
 [B]
                                  2012004433

Manufactured in the United States of America

CPSIA Compliance Information: Batch #WS13PK: For Further Information contact Rosen Publishing, New York, New York at 1-800-237-9932

CONTENTS

Hard-Working Hero 4

World Traveler 6

Tough as a Gator...8

Trophy Winner 10

Tebow-Mania 12

Turning Pro 14

Tebow Time...16

The Winning Throw...18

A Real Champion 20

The Record Book 22

Glossary 23

Index 24

Web Sites 24

HARD-WORKING HERO

Tim Tebow is one of the most popular players in football. He's a star! As quarterback, Tebow led the University of Florida Gators to a national championship. He won the Heisman Trophy for being the best college player in the country. Then he went to the National Football League (NFL) to play quarterback for the Denver Broncos. Tebow has helped Denver come from behind to win many times. He never gives up!

Tebow has been a hero during football games. He has also been a hero off the football field. Tebow is a **role model** for good behavior. He spends lots of time helping people. He's a real leader!

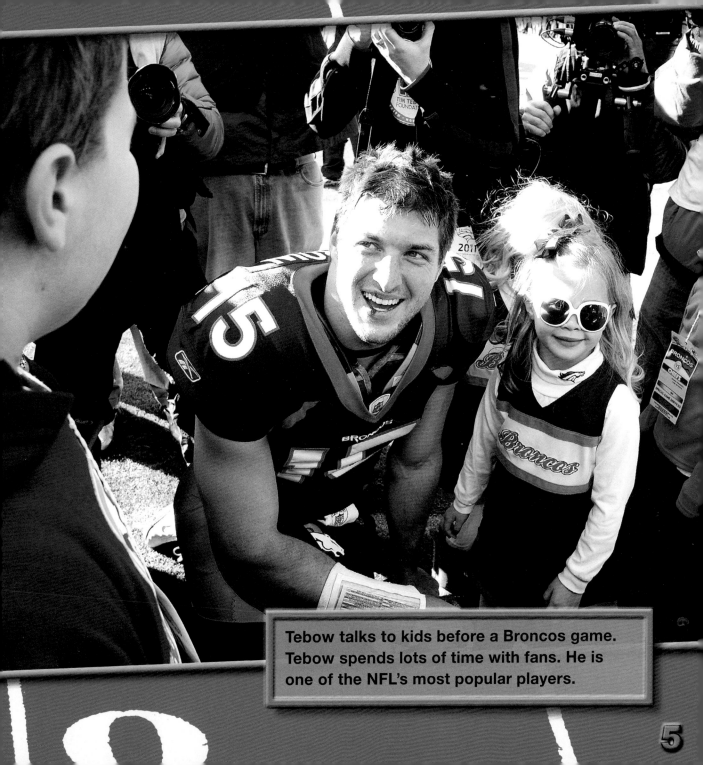

Tebow talks to kids before a Broncos game. Tebow spends lots of time with fans. He is one of the NFL's most popular players.

WORLD TRAVELER

Tebow wasn't born in America. He was born in the Philippines on August 14, 1987. The Philippines are islands in the Pacific Ocean. His parents were Christian **missionaries** there. They lived in the Philippines to share their religious **faith** and help people in need. Tebow's dad built an orphanage in the Philippines. An orphanage is a home for children who don't have parents.

Tebow's family moved to Jacksonville, Florida, when Tebow was three years old. Tebow has four older brothers and sisters. The family lived on a farm. When he was a teenager, Tebow would go back to the Philippines during the summers to share his Christian faith.

Tebow's belief in God is very important to him. Before games at Florida, he wrote Bible verses under his eyes.

TOUGH AS A GATOR

In high school, Tebow was a star quarterback. He was really tough. One time he played a game with a broken bone in his leg. Ouch! Tebow was so good that lots of big colleges **recruited** him. He decided to play for the University of Florida Gators.

Tebow was a **back-up** quarterback during his first year at Florida. But he got to play a lot. He helped the team win the 2006 national championship. The coach used Tebow for both passing and running. Most quarterbacks don't run as well as Tebow. He's hard to tackle. Tebow is 6 foot 3 and about 240 pounds. He's very strong.

Tebow runs the ball against the University of Central Florida during his first season as a Gator. Tebow is hard to tackle.

TROPHY WINNER

Tebow got the job as starting quarterback during his second year at Florida. He played like a superstar! He scored 55 touchdowns running and passing the ball. That set a record for most touchdowns scored by a player in a single season in the Southeastern Conference (SEC). Tebow played so well in 2007 that he won the Heisman Trophy award for best player in the country.

Tebow's third year at Florida was even better. He led the Gators to a national championship. They beat the Oklahoma Sooners 24-14 in the championship **bowl** game. Tebow became a hero in the state of Florida.

Tebow poses with his Heisman Trophy award. In 2007, Tebow won the award for being the best college player in the country.

11

TEBOW-MANIA

At the end of his third year of college, Tebow had a tough decision to make. Should he turn **professional** and go to the NFL? Or should he stay at Florida and try to win another championship? Tebow decided to stay in school and finish his **senior** year.

Tebow played well his final year. His team didn't make it to the national championship. But Tebow finished his college career with a great game. Florida beat Cincinnati 51-24 in a bowl game. It was Tebow's last game as a Gator, and he scored four touchdowns. During his years at Florida, Tebow had one of the best careers in college football history!

Tebow celebrates after beating Cincinnati in the Sugar Bowl. Tebow got to end his career at Florida with a victory.

TURNING PRO

Everyone knew Tebow could run well. But could he throw well enough to be a professional quarterback? Some people didn't think so, and that made Tebow work even harder. Tebow trained to improve his throwing skills. The Denver Broncos liked what they saw. They chose Tebow in the first round of the **draft.**

Tebow mainly played as a back-up during his first season with the Broncos. The next year, in 2011, the Broncos got off to a bad start. The team lost four out of five games. The coach then decided to give Tebow a chance to start as quarterback. That turned out to be a good decision.

Tebow runs for a touchdown against the New York Jets during his first year as a Bronco. He ran for six touchdowns his rookie year.

TEBOW TIME

In Tebow's first game as a starter, the Broncos were losing 15-0 to the Miami Dolphins. There were only three minutes left in the game. But guess who came to the rescue? Tim Tebow! He threw for two touchdowns and led the Broncos to an **overtime** victory. A few weeks later, the Broncos were playing the New York Jets. The Broncos were losing 13-10 with only six minutes left to play. Tebow led them down the field. Then with one minute left, he ran for a 20 yard touchdown. The Broncos won again!

Tebow never gives up. In five different games, Denver was losing in the fourth quarter, and Tebow helped them come back and win. He's the **comeback** king!

Tebow runs for the game-winning touchdown against the New York Jets in 2011. He scored in the final minute of the game.

THE WINNING THROW

With Tebow as their new starting quarterback, the Broncos won enough games to reach the playoffs. But they faced a tough opponent in their first playoff game—the Pittsburgh Steelers. It was a close game that went into overtime. On the very first play of overtime, Tebow threw a long pass to his wide receiver. It was a perfect throw, and the receiver ran all the way for a touchdown. The Broncos beat the Steelers!

Denver lost their next playoff game to the New England Patriots. But Tebow still had a good season. He proved that he can win big games in the NFL. He has the heart of a champion.

Tebow gets ready to throw a winning pass during overtime against the Pittsburgh Steelers. It was an 80-yard play.

A REAL CHAMPION

When Tebow was a young boy, one of his favorite sayings was, "Hard work beats talent when talent doesn't work hard." Tebow has always worked hard to become the best player he can be. He also works hard off the football field. He spends a lot of time helping poor and sick people, especially children. Tebow also spends lots of time talking about his belief in God. His Christian faith is very important to him.

Tebow is a hero to many people. He has won over the fans in Denver. In March 2012, Tebow was traded to the New York Jets. As a Jet, he is sure to gain even more fans.

Tebow prays before a game. Tebow often gets down on one knee to pray. He likes to share his Christian faith with people.

TIM TEBOW
2007 HEISMAN TROPHY WINNER
UNIVERSITY OF FLORIDA
QUARTERBACK

	Passing Stats	Rushing Stats
Years	Yards/Touchdowns	Yards/Touchdowns
2006-2009	9,285 yds./88 TDs	2,947 yds./57 TDs
University of Florida		

FUN FACTS

Tebow became the first sophomore (a second-year college student) to win the Heisman Trophy award.

In 2007, Tebow became the first college player to throw for 20 touchdowns and run for 20 touchdowns in a single season.

TIM TEBOW
BIRTH DATE: 8–14–87
BIRTHPLACE: MAKATI CITY, PHILIPPINES
HEIGHT: 6' 3"   WEIGHT: 240 LBS.

		Passing Stats	Rushing Stats
Year	Team	Yards/Touchdowns	Yards/Touchdowns
2010	BRONCOS	654 yds./5 TDs	227 yds./6 TDs
2011	BRONCOS	1,729 yds./12 TDs	660 yds./6 TDs
Career		2,383 yds./17 TDs	887 yds./12 TDs

GLOSSARY

BACK-UP (BAK-up) To be the second choice for something.

BOWL (Bole) A college football game played after the regular season is over.

COMEBACK (kum-bak) To beat a team after being behind in the score.

DRAFT (Draft) A time when the NFL chooses new players for the teams.

FAITH (Fayth) Belief in God.

MISSIONARIES (MISH-un-air-ees) People who share their religion.

OVERTIME (O-vur-time) When a game is tied and teams play extra time to decide the winner.

PROFESSIONAL (pruh-FESH-u-nul) Someone who gets paid money to play sports.

RECRUIT (re-KRUTE) When teams try to get a player to join their team.

ROLE MODEL (ROLE-MOD-ul) Someone who behaves well; someone you want to be like.

SENIOR (SEEN-yur) A student who is in his last year of college.

INDEX

C
championship, 8, 10, 12

D
draft, 14

F
faith, 6, 20, 21
Florida, 4, 7, 8, 9, 10, 12, 13, 22

H
Heisman Trophy, 10, 11, 22

M
missionaries, 6

N
National Football League (NFL), 4, 5, 12, 18

O
overtime, 18, 19

P
passing, 8, 10
Philippines 6, 22

playoffs, 18

Q
quarterback, 4, 8, 14, 18

S
Southeastern Conference (SEC), 10
Super Bowl, 20

T
touchdown, 10, 15, 16, 17, 22

WEB SITES

Due to the changing nature of Internet links, PowerKids Press has developed an online list of Web sites related to the subject of this book. This site is updated regularly. Please use this link to access the list:
www.powerkidslinks.com/frs/Tebow/